THE NuTcracker
FOR SOLO FINGERSTYLE GUITAR

ISBN 978-1-4584-0805-1

HAL•LEONARD®
CORPORATION

7777 W. BLUEMOUND RD. P.O. BOX 13819 MILWAUKEE, WI 53213

In Australia Contact:
Hal Leonard Australia Pty. Ltd.
4 Lentara Court
Cheltenham, Victoria, 3192 Australia
Email: ausadmin@halleonard.com.au

Visit Hal Leonard Online at
www.halleonard.com

CONTENTS

Overture

By Pyotr Il'yich Tchaikovsky

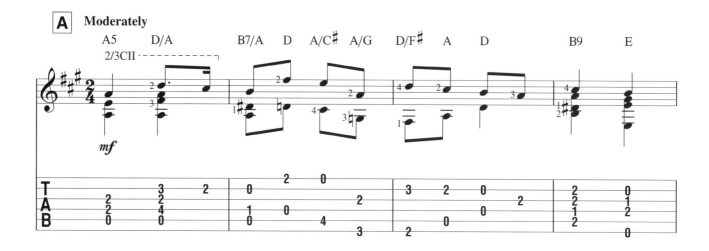

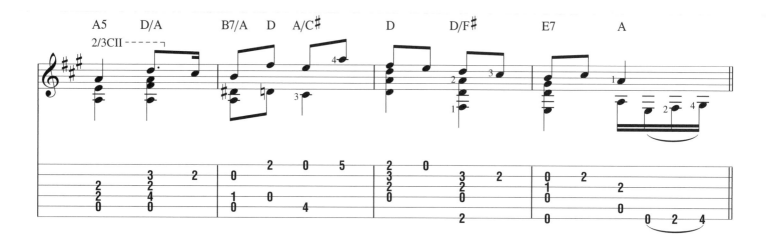

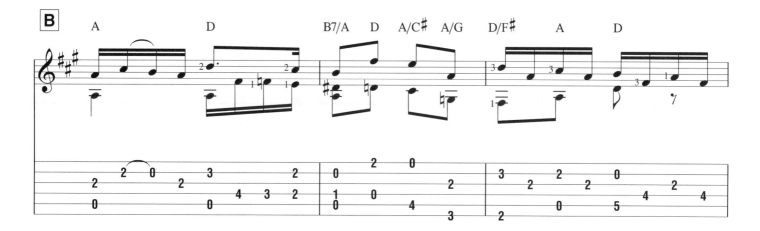

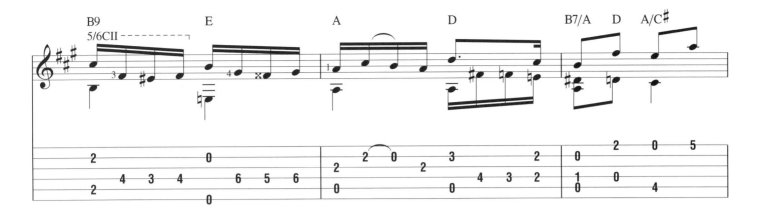

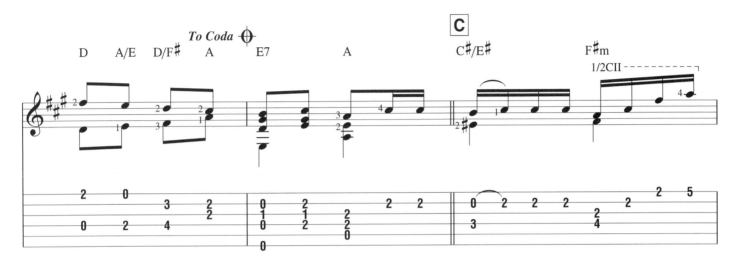

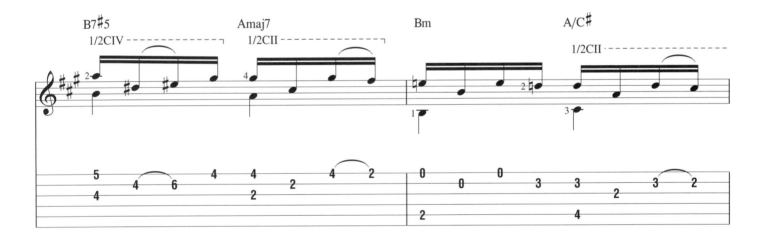

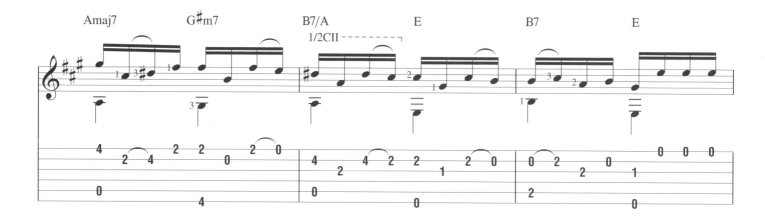

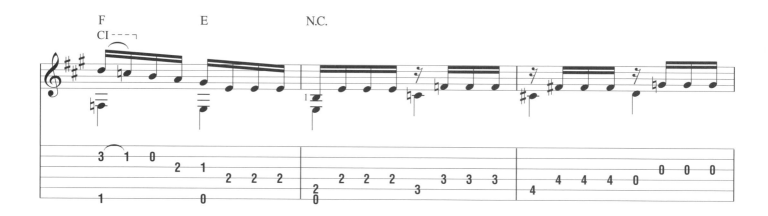

Chinese Dance
"Tea"
By Pyotr Il'yich Tchaikovsky

Drop D tuning:
(low to high) D-A-D-G-B-E

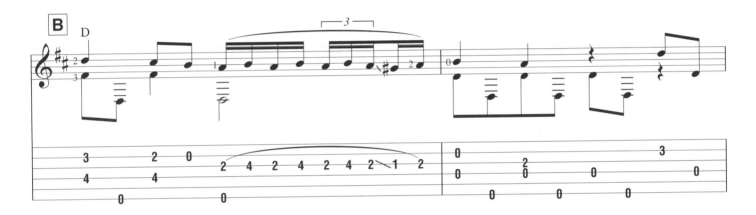

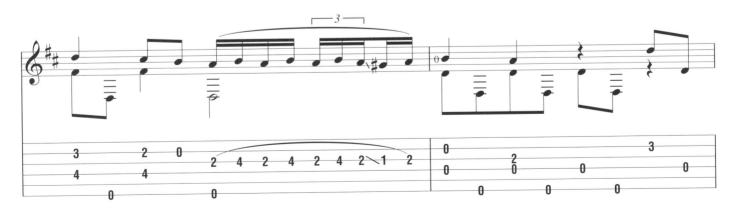

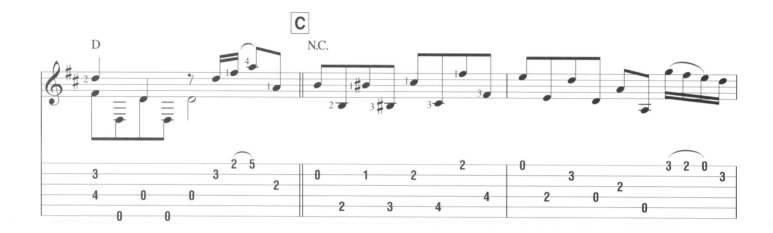

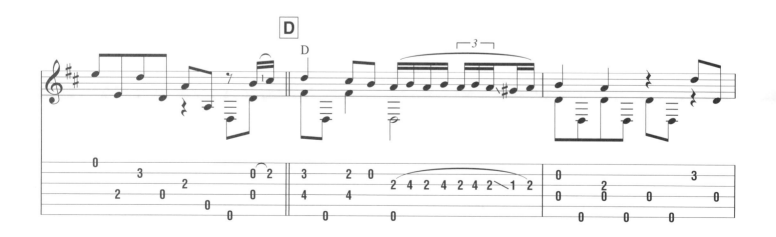

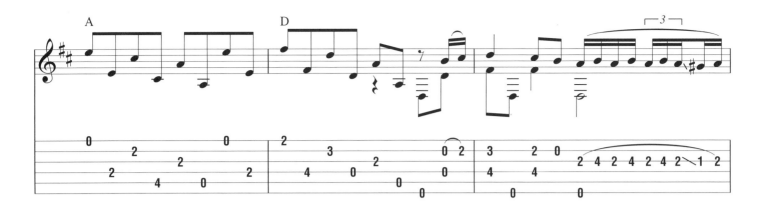

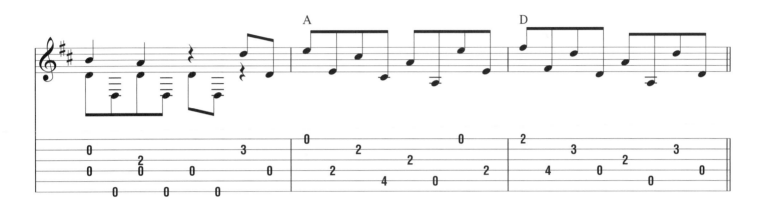

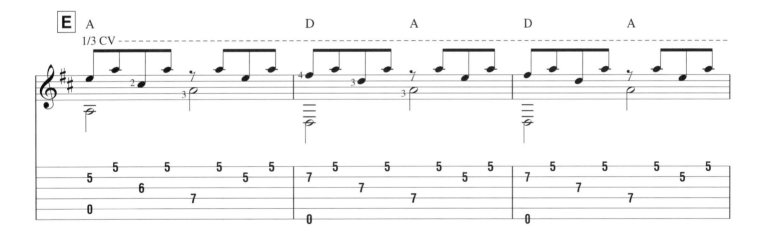

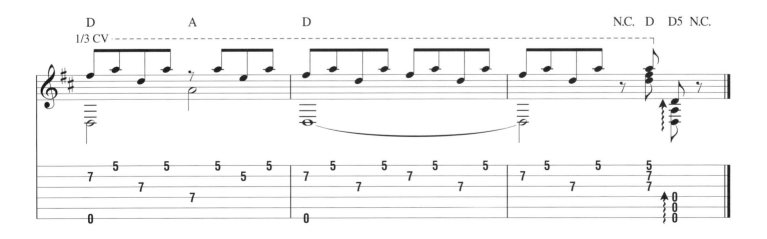

March

By Pyotr Il'yich Tchaikovsky

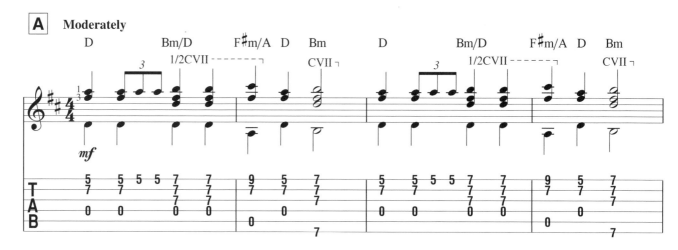

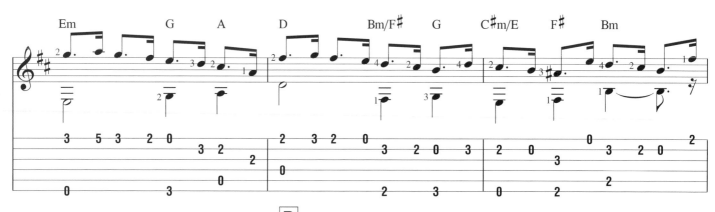

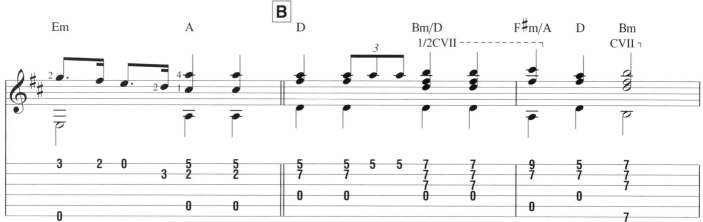

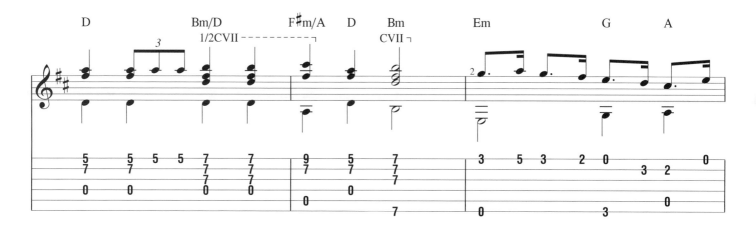

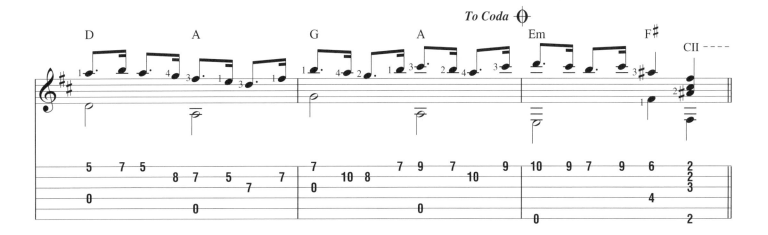

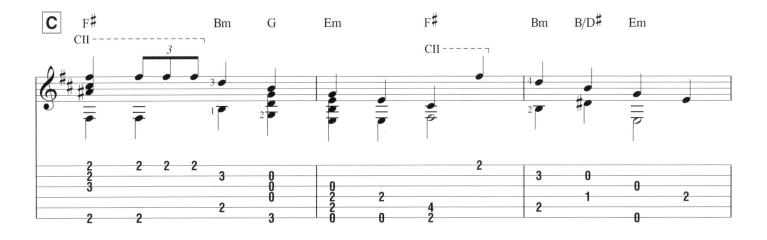

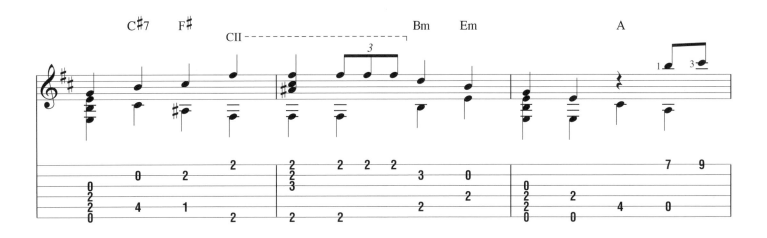

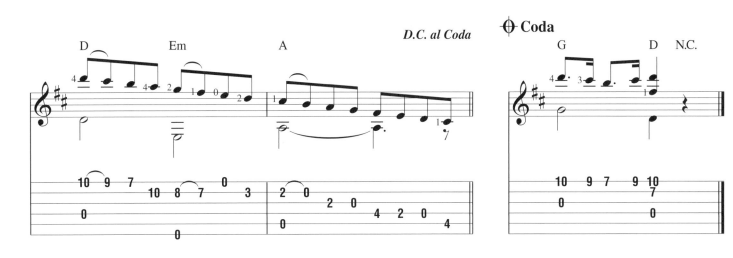

Dance of the Sugar Plum Fairy

By Pyotr Il'yich Tchaikovsky

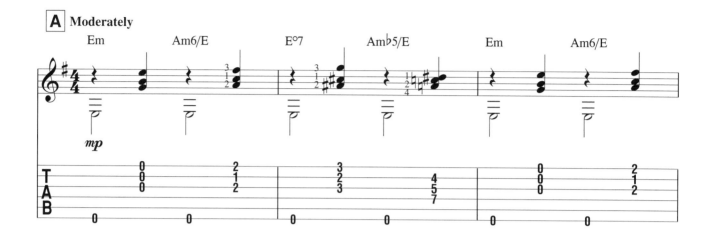

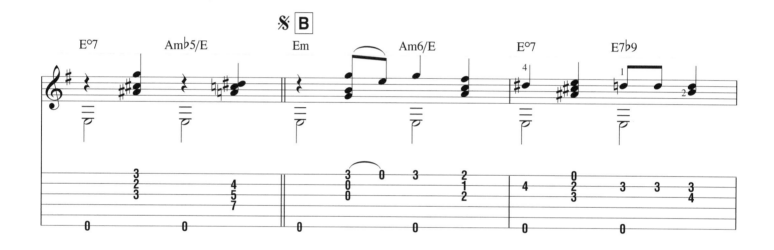

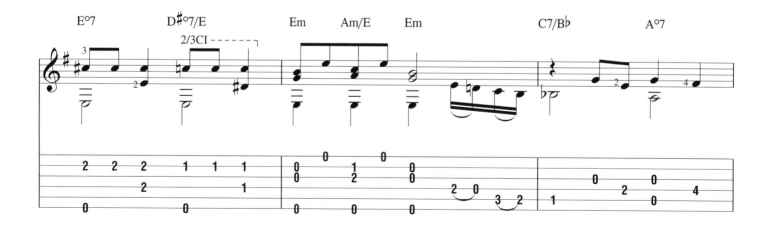

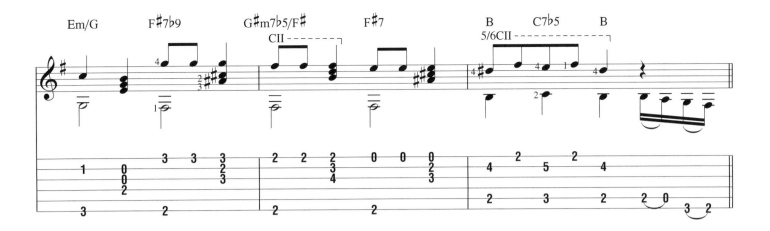

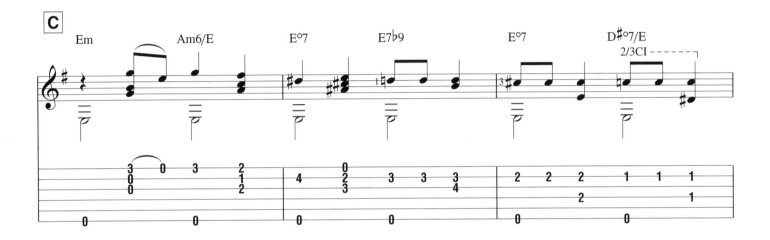

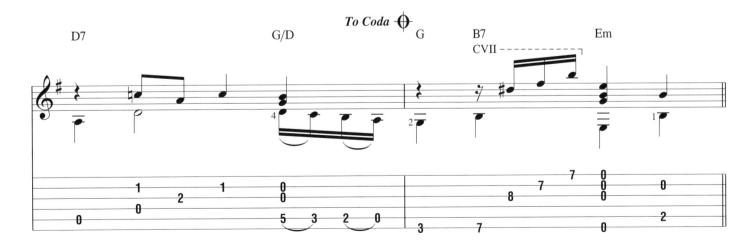

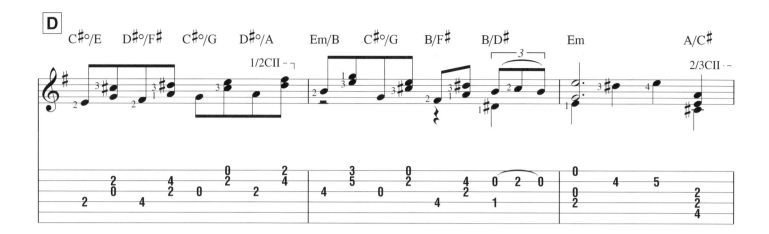

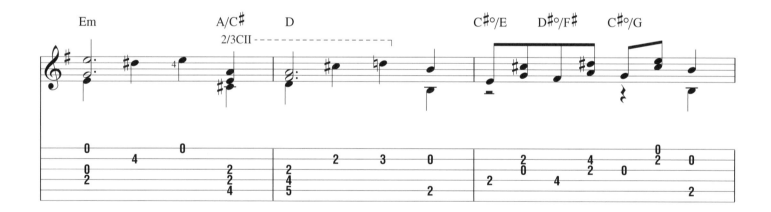

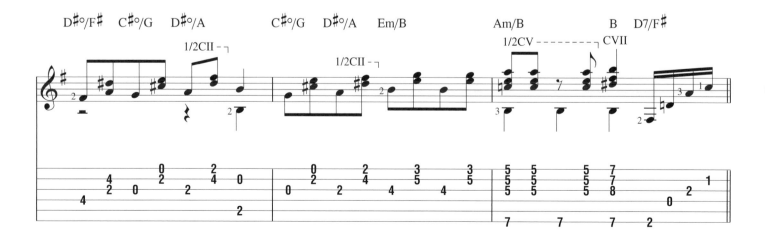

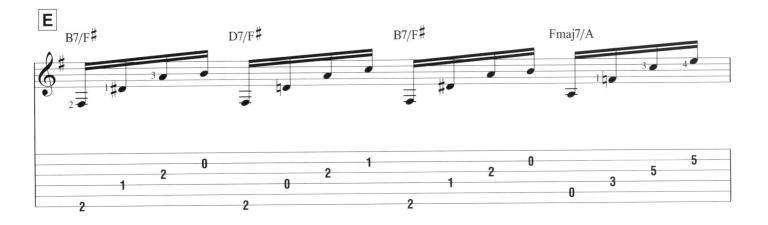

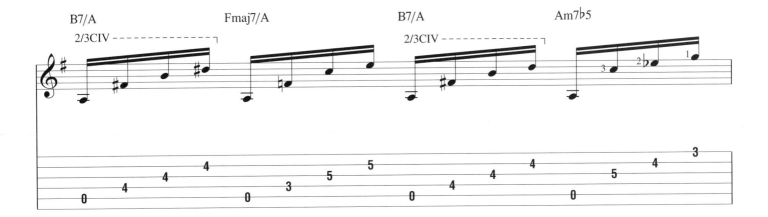

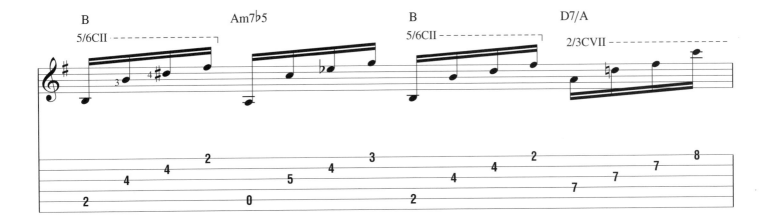

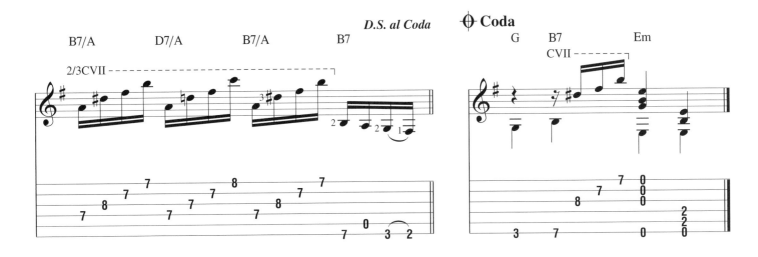

Russian Dance
"Trepak"
By Pytor Il'yich Tchaikovsky

Drop D tuning:
(low to high) D-A-D-G-B-E

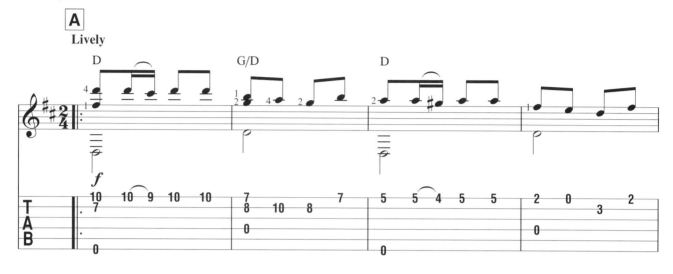

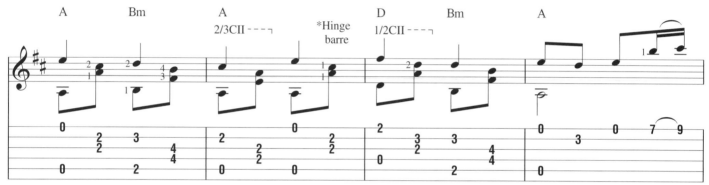

*w/ fleshy side of finger above knuckle.

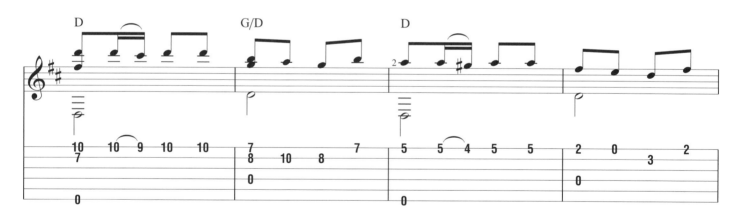

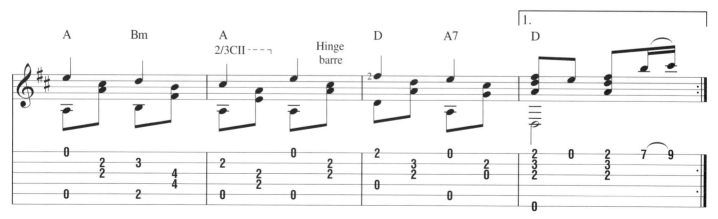

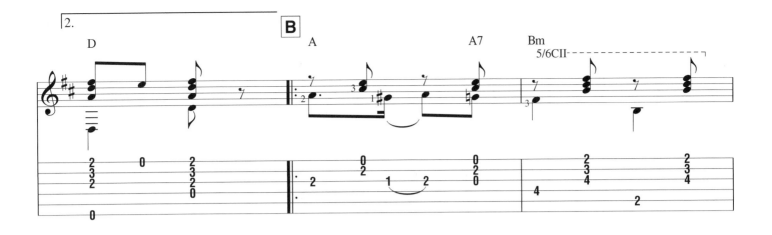

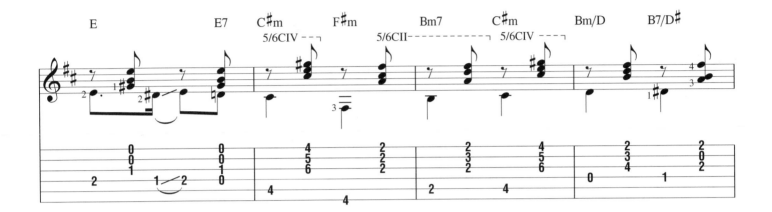

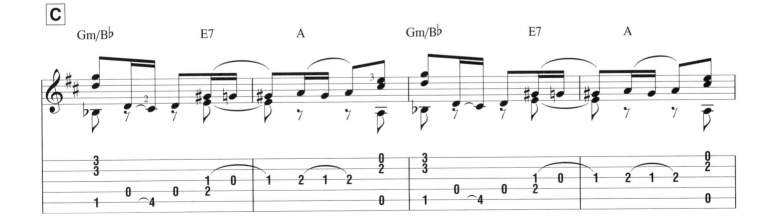

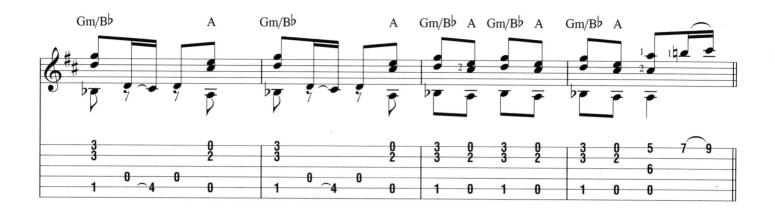

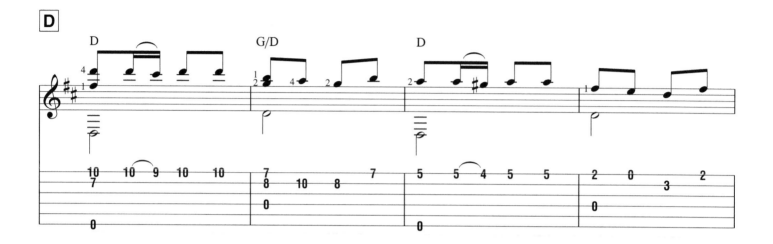

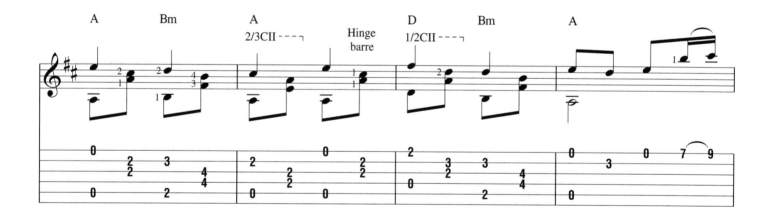

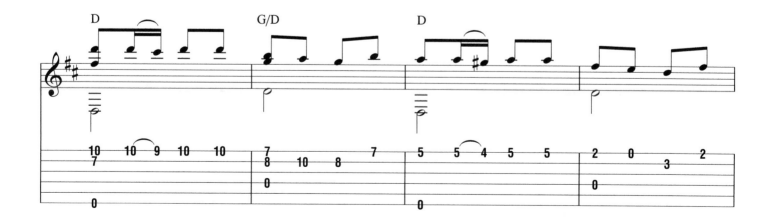

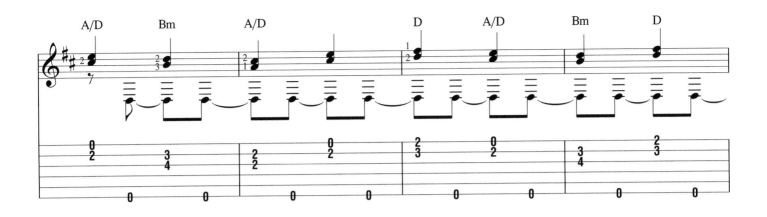

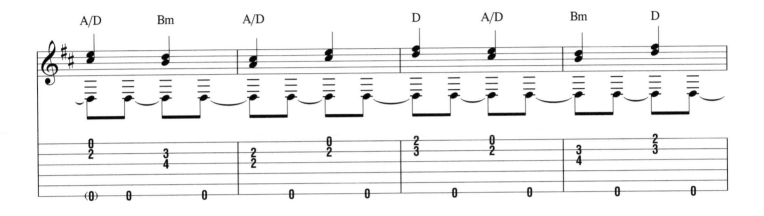

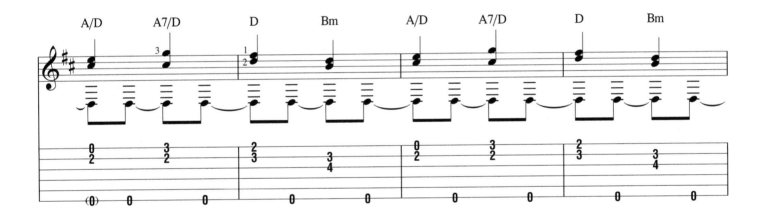

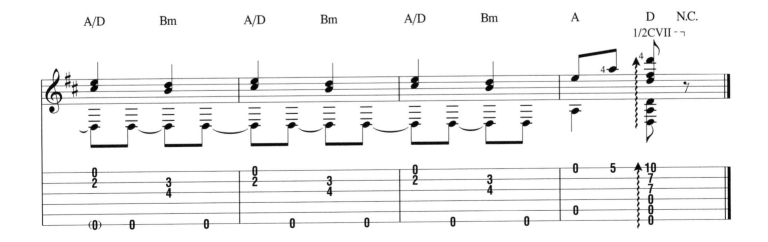

Arabian Dance
"Coffee"
By Pyotr Il'yich Tchaikovsky

Drop D tuning:
(low to high) D-A-D-G-B-E

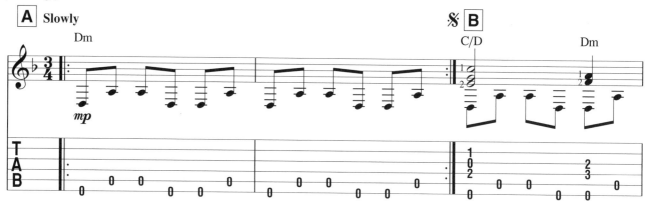

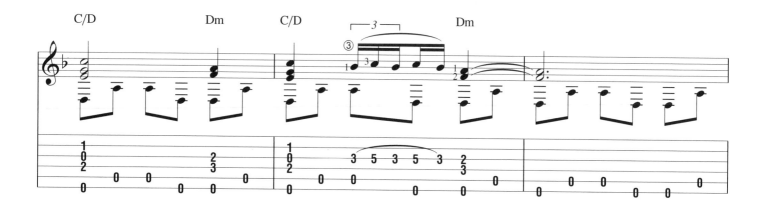

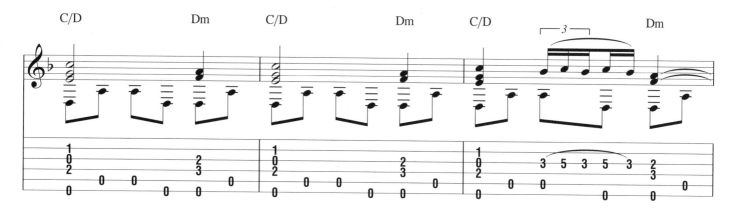

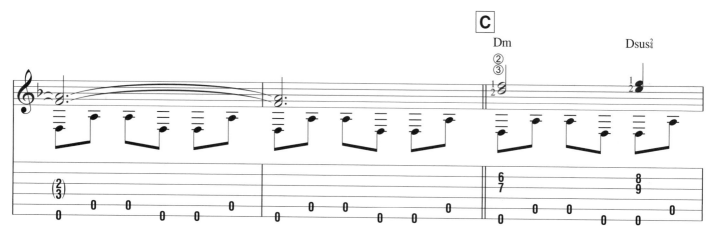

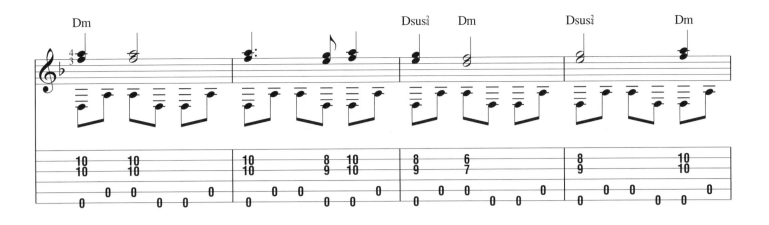

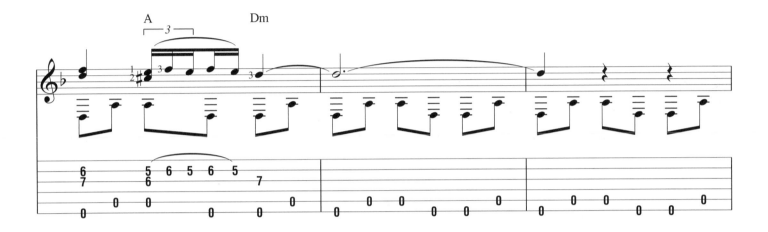

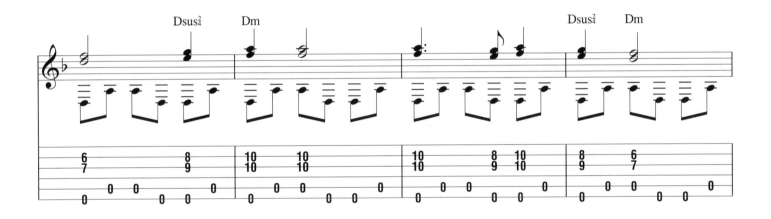

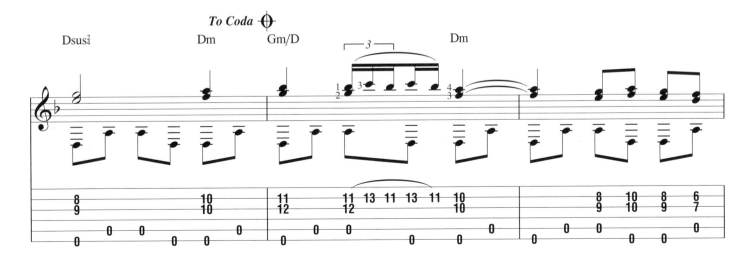

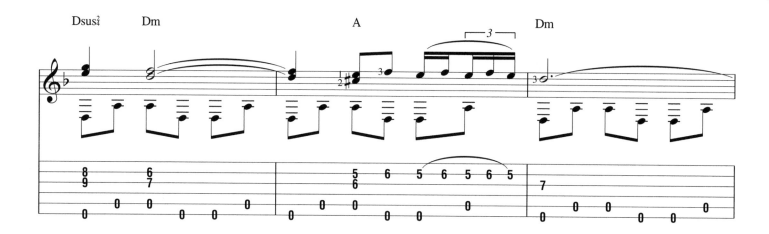

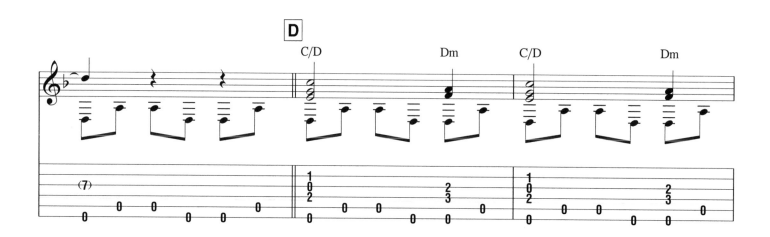

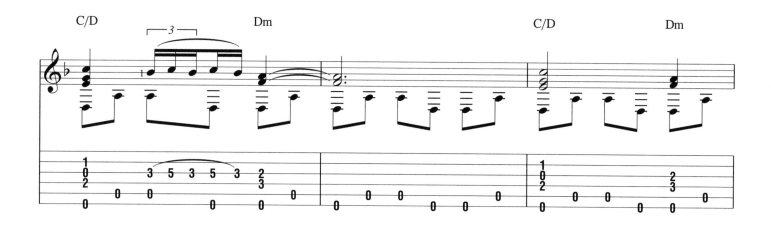

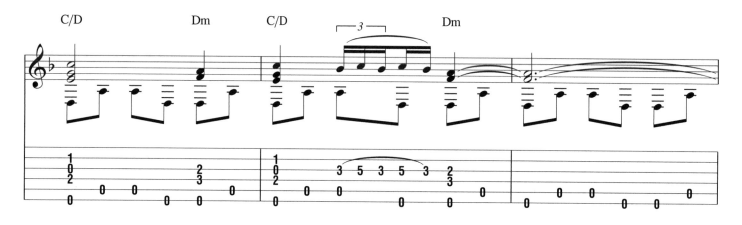

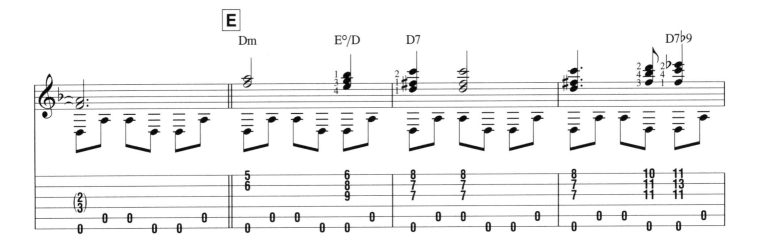

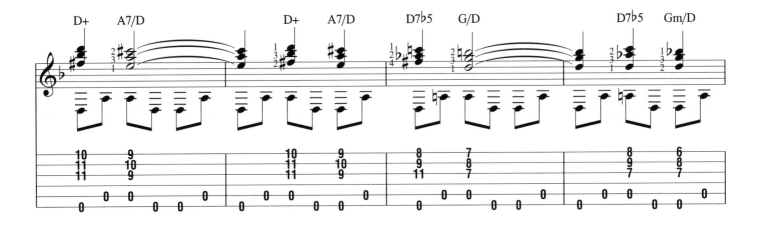

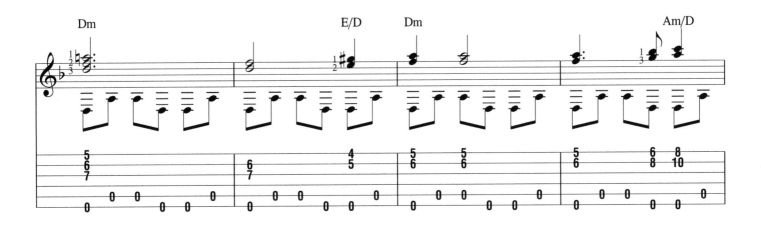

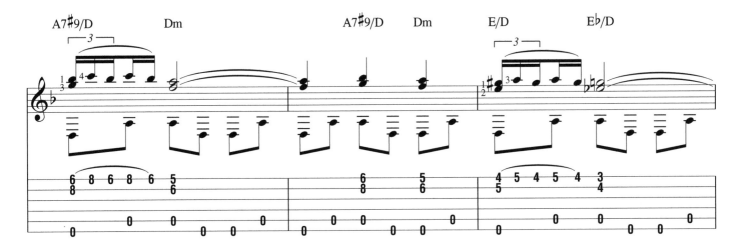

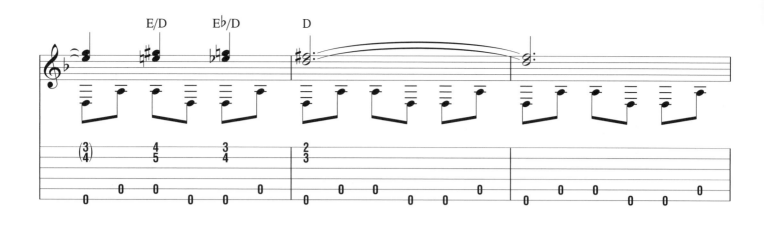

D.S. al Coda   ⊕ **Coda**

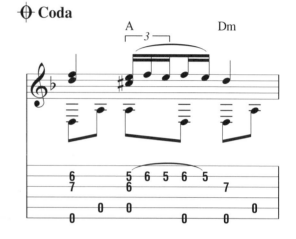
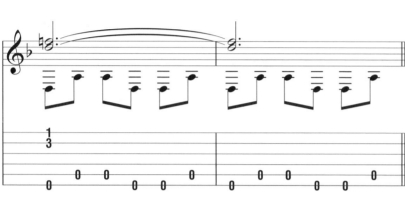

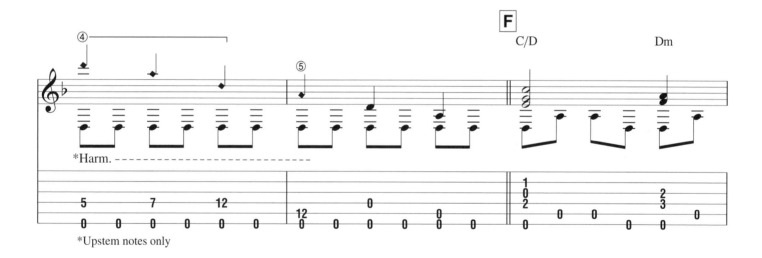

Harm.

*Upstem notes only

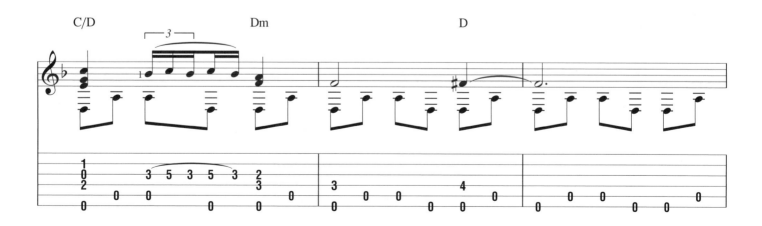

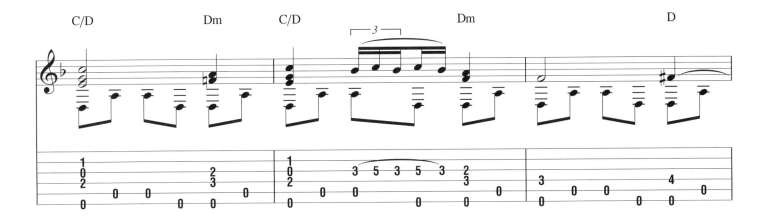

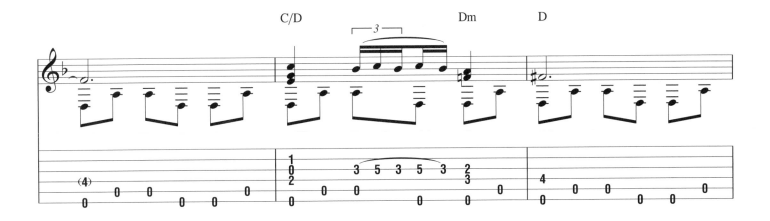

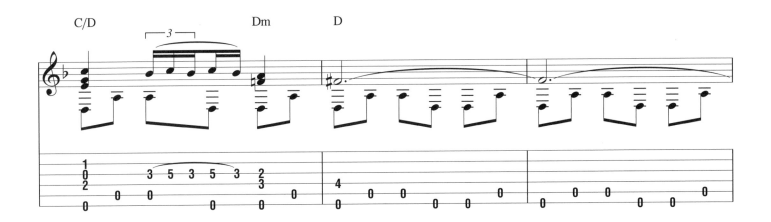

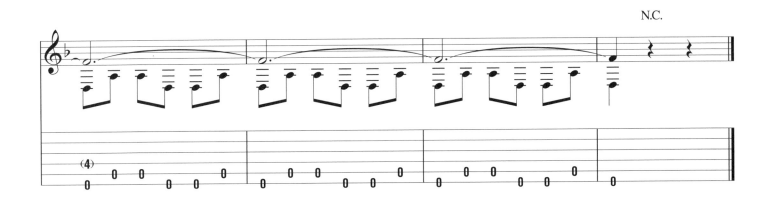

The Waltz of the Flowers

By Pyotr Il'yich Tchaikovsky

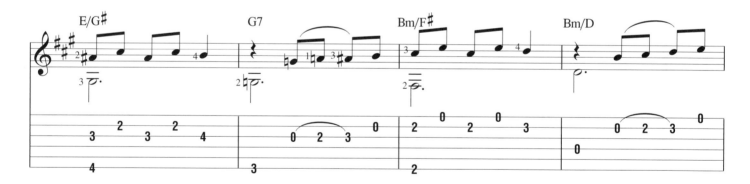

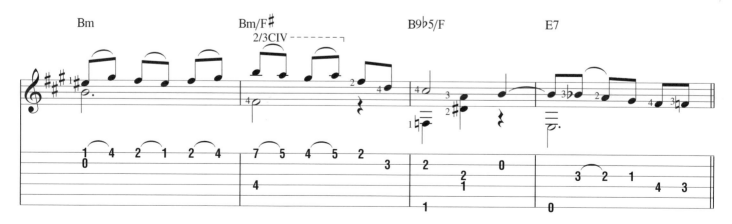

B

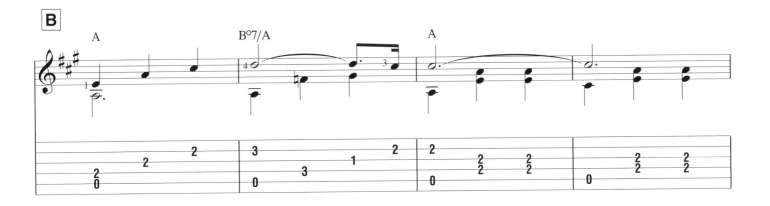

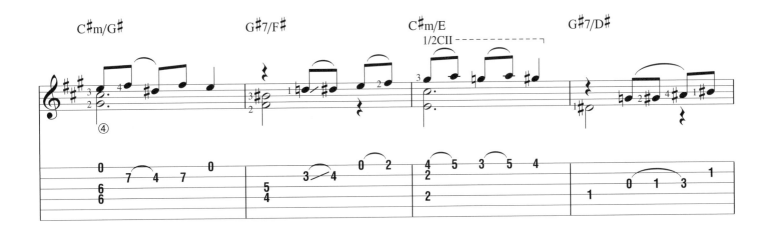

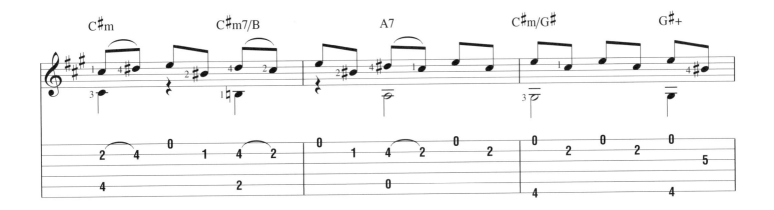

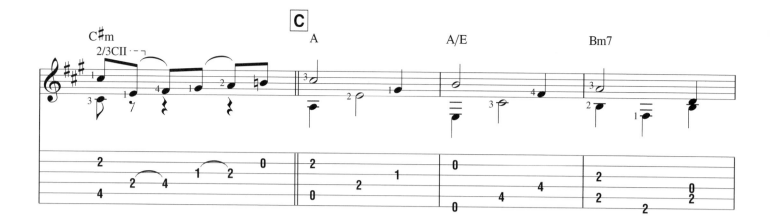

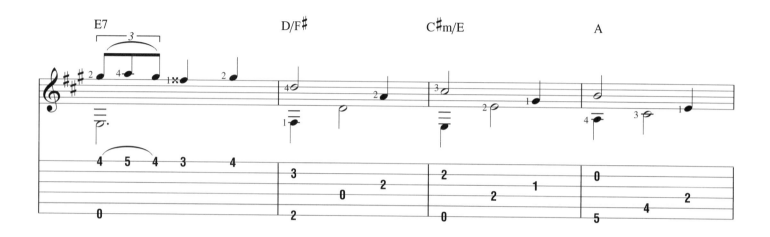

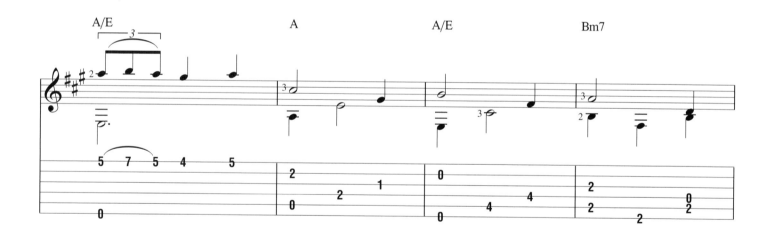

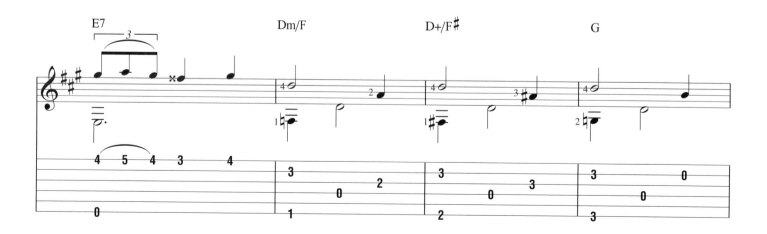

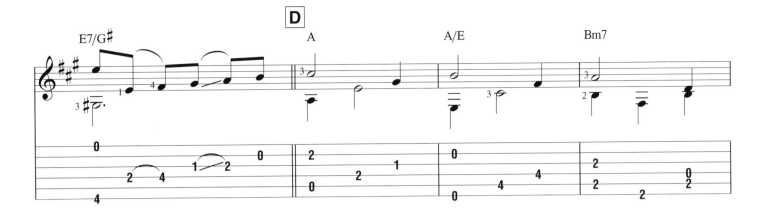

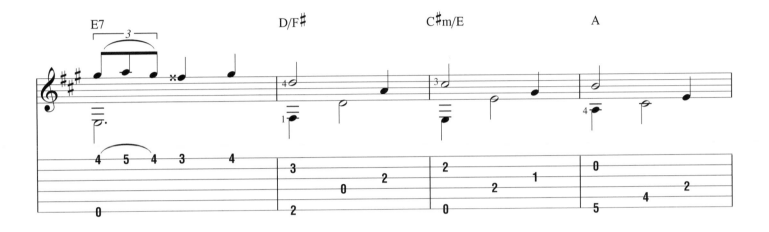

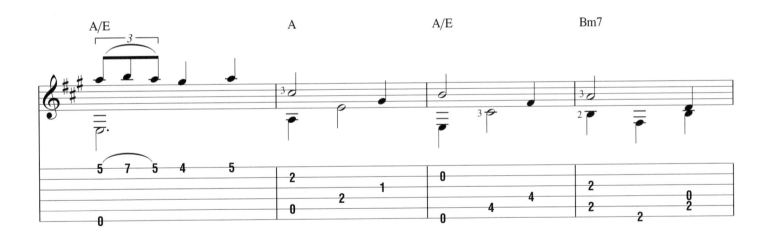

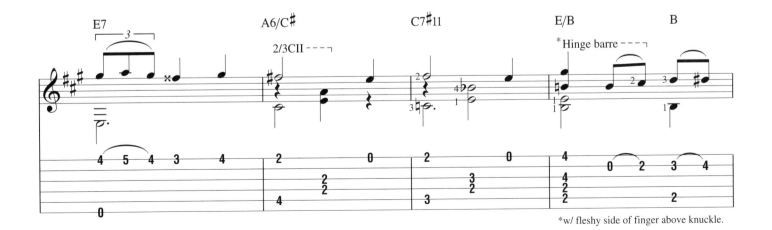

*w/ fleshy side of finger above knuckle.

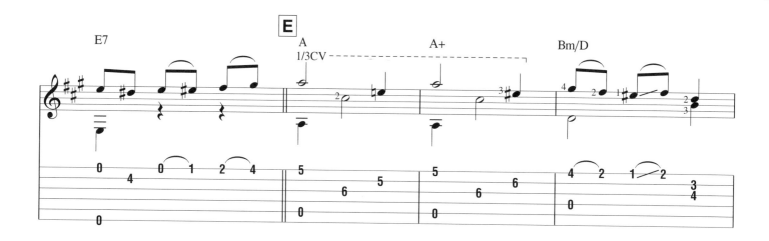

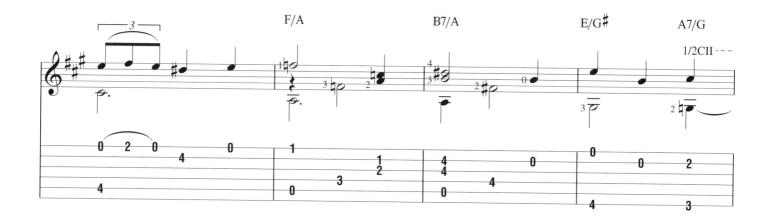

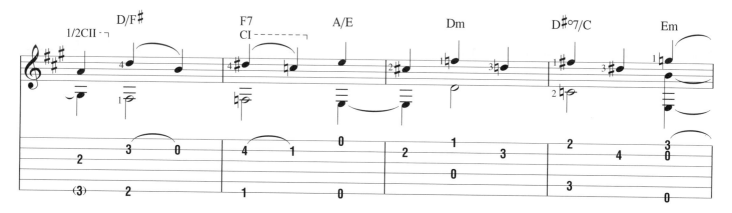

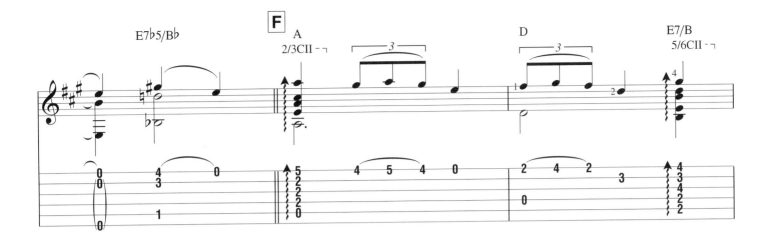

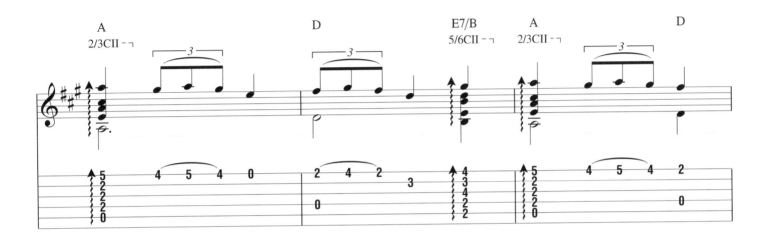

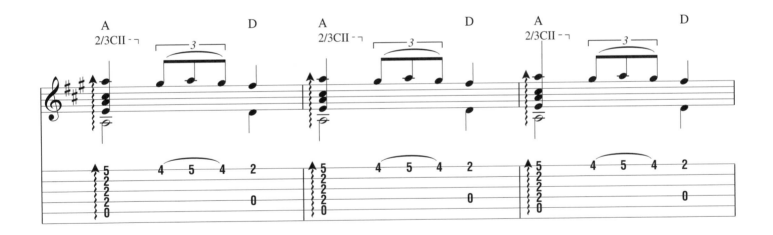

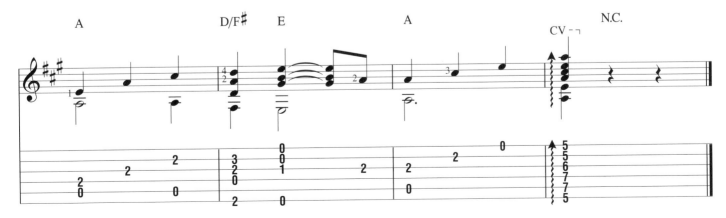

Dance of the Reed-Flutes

By Pyotr Il'yich Tchaikovsky

Drop D tuning:
(low to high) D-A-D-G-B-E

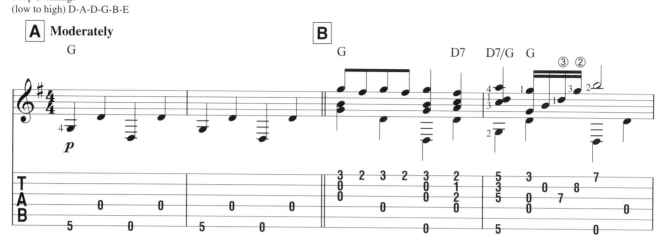

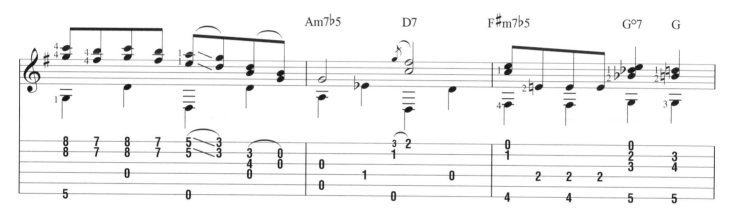

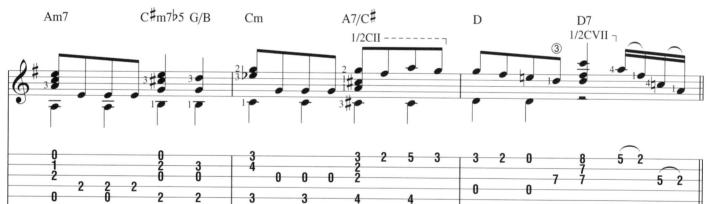

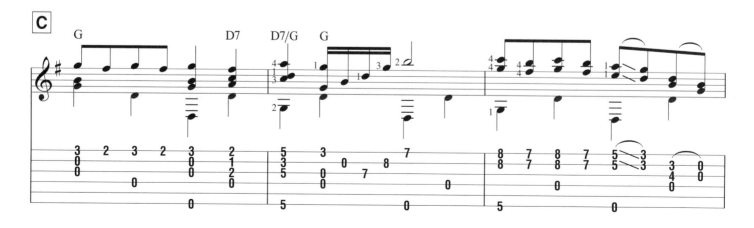

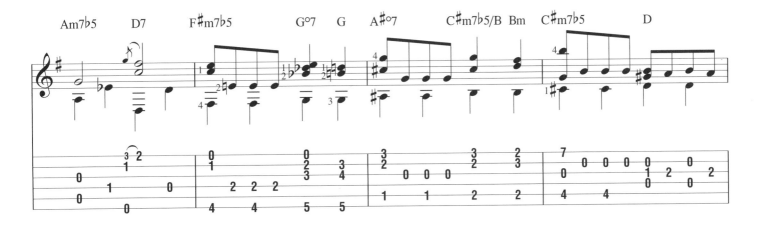

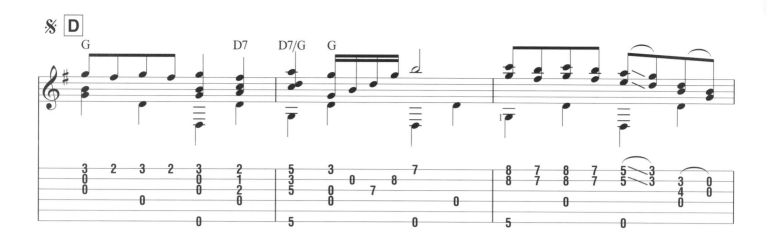

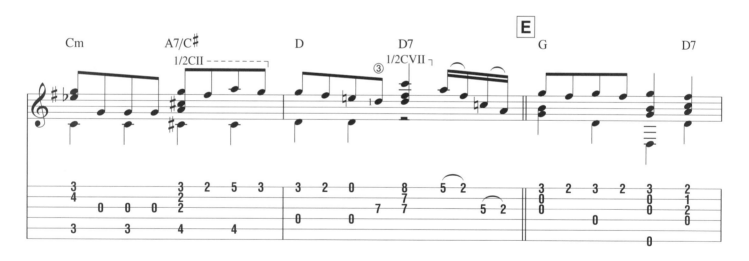

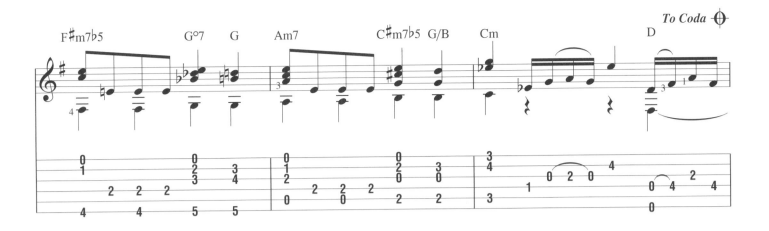

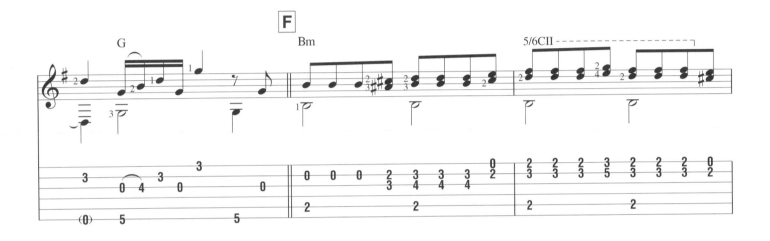

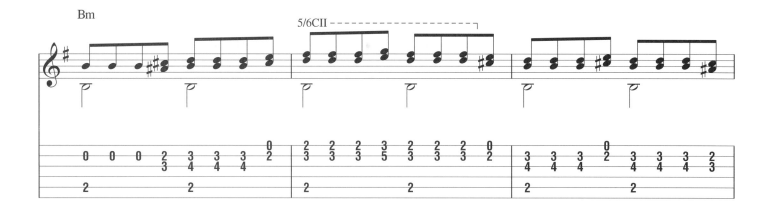

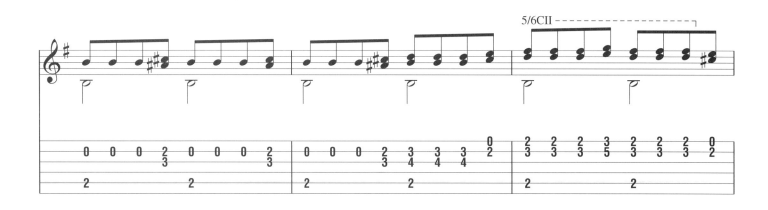

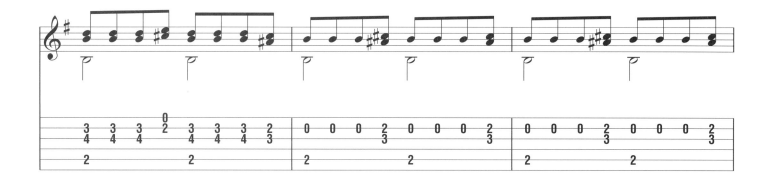

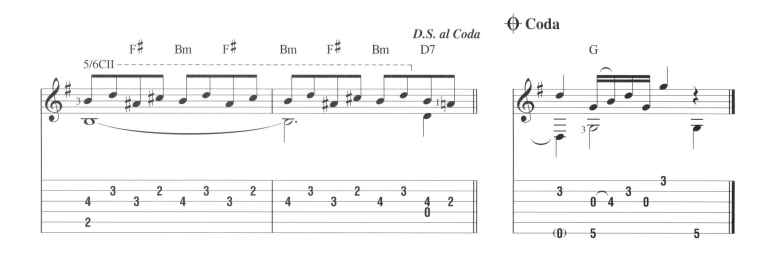

CLASSICAL GUITAR PUBLICATIONS FROM HAL LEONARD

THE BEATLES FOR CLASSICAL GUITAR

Includes 20 solos from big Beatles hits arranged for classical guitar, complete with left-hand and right-hand fingering. Songs include: All My Loving • And I Love Her • Can't Buy Me Love • Fool on the Hill • From a Window • Hey Jude • If I Fell • Let It Be • Michelle • Norwegian Wood • Obla Di • Ticket to Ride • Yesterday • and more. Features arrangements and an introduction by Joe Washington, as well as his helpful hints on classical technique and detailed notes on how to play each song. The book also covers parts and specifications of the classical guitar, tuning, and Joe's "Strata System" – an easy-reading system applied to chord diagrams.

_____ 00699237 Classical Guitar $19.99

MATTEO CARCASSI – 25 MELODIC AND PROGRESSIVE STUDIES, OP. 60
arr. Paul Henry

One of Carcassi's (1792-1853) most famous collections of classical guitar music – indispensable for the modern guitarist's musical and technical development. Performed by Paul Henry. 49-minute audio accompaniment.

_____ 00696506 Book/CD Pack $17.95

CLASSICAL & FINGERSTYLE GUITAR TECHNIQUES INCLUDES TAB
by David Oakes • Musicians Institute

This Master Class with MI instructor David Oakes is aimed at any electric or acoustic guitarist who wants a quick, thorough grounding in the essentials of classical and fingerstyle technique. Topics covered include: arpeggios and scales, free stroke and rest stroke, P-i scale technique, three-to-a-string patterns, natural and artificial harmonics, tremolo and rasgueado, and more. The book includes 12 intensive lessons for right and left hand in standard notation & tab, and the CD features 92 solo acoustic tracks.

_____ 00695171 Book/CD Pack $17.99

CLASSICAL GUITAR CHRISTMAS COLLECTION INCLUDES TAB

Includes classical guitar arrangements in standard notation and tablature for more than two dozen beloved carols: Angels We Have Heard on High • Auld Lang Syne • Ave Maria • Away in a Manger • Canon in D • The First Noel • God Rest Ye Merry, Gentlemen • Hark! the Herald Angels Sing • I Saw Three Ships • Jesu, Joy of Man's Desiring • Joy to the World • O Christmas Tree • O Holy Night • Silent Night • What Child Is This? • and more.

_____ 00699493 Guitar Solo $9.95

CLASSICAL GUITAR WEDDING INCLUDES TAB

Perfect for players hired to perform for someone's big day, this songbook features 16 classical wedding favorites arranged for solo guitar in standard notation and tablature. Includes: Air on the G String • Ave Maria • Bridal Chorus • Canon in D • Jesu, Joy of Man's Desiring • Minuet • Sheep May Safely Graze • Wedding March • and more.

_____ 00699563 Solo Guitar with Tab $10.95

CLASSICAL MASTERPIECES FOR GUITAR INCLUDES TAB

27 works by Bach, Beethoven, Handel, Mendelssohn, Mozart and more transcribed with standard notation and tablature. Now anyone can enjoy classical material regardless of their guitar background. Also features stay-open binding.

_____ 00699312 ....$12.95

CLASSICAL THEMES INCLUDES TAB

20 beloved classical themes arranged for easy guitar in large-size notes (with the note names in the note heads) and tablature. Includes: Air on the G String (Bach) • Ave Maria (Schubert) • Für Elise (Beethoven) • In the Hall of the Mountain King (Grieg) • Jesu, Joy of Man's Desiring (Bach) • Largo (Handel) • Ode to Joy (Beethoven) • Pomp and Circumstance (Elgar) • and more. Ideal for beginning or vision-impaired players.

_____ 00699272 E-Z Play Guitar.........................$9.95

MASTERWORKS FOR GUITAR INCLUDES TAB
Over 60 Favorites from Four Centuries
World's Great Classical Music

Dozens of classical masterpieces: Allemande • Bourree • Canon in D • Jesu, Joy of Man's Desiring • Lagrima • Malaguena • Mazurka • Piano Sonata No. 14 in C# Minor (Moonlight) Op. 27 No. 2 First Movement Theme • Ode to Joy • Prelude No. I (Well-Tempered Clavier).

_____ 00699503 ....$16.95

FOR MORE INFORMATION, SEE YOUR LOCAL MUSIC DEALER, OR WRITE TO:

HAL•LEONARD® CORPORATION
7777 W. BLUEMOUND RD. P.O. BOX 13819 MILWAUKEE, WI 53213

Visit Hal Leonard Online at **www.halleonard.com**

A MODERN APPROACH TO CLASSICAL GUITAR
by Charles Duncan

This multi-volume method was developed to allow students to study the art of classical guitar within a new, more contemporary framework. For private, class or self-instruction. Book One incorporates chord frames and symbols, as well as a recording to assist in tuning and to provide accompaniments for at-home practice. Book One also introduces beginning fingerboard technique and music theory. Book Two and Three build upon the techniques learned in Book One.

_____ 00695114 Book 1 – Book Only...............$6.99
_____ 00695113 Book 1 – Book/CD Pack $10.99
_____ 00695116 Book 2 – Book Only...............$6.95
_____ 00695115 Book 2 – Book/CD Pack $10.95
_____ 00699202 Book 3 – Book Only...............$7.95
_____ 00695117 Book 3 – Book/CD Pack $10.95
_____ 00695119 Composite Book/CD Pack.....$29.99

ANDRES SEGOVIA – 20 STUDIES FOR GUITAR
Sor/Segovia

20 studies for the classical guitar written by Beethoven's contemporary, Fernando Sor, revised, edited and fingered by the great classical guitarist Andres Segovia. These essential repertoire pieces continue to be used by teachers and students to build solid classical technique. Features a 50-minute demonstration CD.

_____ 00695012 Book/CD Pack $18.95
_____ 00006363 Book Only $7.95

THE FRANCISCO TÁRREGA COLLECTION INCLUDES TAB
edited and performed by Paul Henry

Considered the father of modern classical guitar, Francisco Tárrega revolutionized guitar technique and composed a wealth of music that will be a cornerstone of classical guitar repertoire for centuries to come. This unique book/CD pack features 14 of his most outstanding pieces in standard notation and tab, edited and performed on CD by virtuoso Paul Henry. Includes: Adelita • Capricho Árabe • Estudio Brillante • Grand Jota • Lágrima • Malagueña • María • Recuerdos de la Alhambra • Tango • and more, plus bios of Tárrega and Henry.

_____ 00698993 Book/CD Pack $19.99

Prices, contents and availability subject to change without notice.

FINGERPICKING GUITAR BOOKS

Hone your fingerpicking skills with these great songbooks featuring solo guitar arrangements in standard notation and tablature. The arrangements in these books are carefully written for intermediate-level guitarists. Each song combines melody and harmony in one superb guitar fingerpicking arrangement. Each book also includes an introduction to basic fingerstyle guitar.

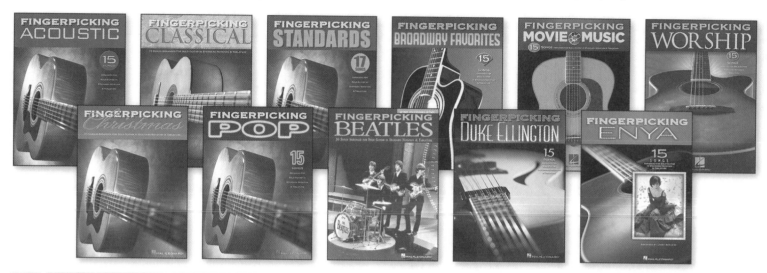

FINGERPICKING ACOUSTIC
00699614......$10.99

FINGERPICKING ACOUSTIC ROCK
00699764......$9.99

FINGERPICKING BACH
00699793......$8.95

FINGERPICKING BALLADS
00699717......$9.99

FINGERPICKING BEATLES
00699049......$19.99

FINGERPICKING BROADWAY FAVORITES
00699843......$9.99

FINGERPICKING BROADWAY HITS
00699838......$7.99

FINGERPICKING CELTIC FOLK
00701148......$7.99

FINGERPICKING CHILDREN'S SONGS
00699712......$9.99

FINGERPICKING CHRISTMAS
00699599......$8.95

FINGERPICKING CHRISTMAS CLASSICS
00701695......$7.99

FINGERPICKING CLASSICAL
00699620......$8.95

FINGERPICKING COUNTRY
00699687......$9.99

FINGERPICKING DISNEY
00699711......$9.95

FINGERPICKING DUKE ELLINGTON
00699845......$9.99

FINGERPICKING ENYA
00701161......$9.99

FINGERPICKING GOSPEL
00701059......$7.99

FINGERPICKING HYMNS
00699688......$8.95

FINGERPICKING LATIN STANDARDS
00699837......$7.99

FINGERPICKING ANDREW LLOYD WEBBER
00699839......$9.99

FINGERPICKING LOVE SONGS
00699841......$7.99

FINGERPICKING LULLABYES
00701276......$9.99

FINGERPICKING MOVIE MUSIC
00699919......$9.99

FINGERPICKING MOZART
00699794......$8.95

FINGERPICKING POP
00699615......$9.99

FINGERPICKING PRAISE
00699714......$8.95

FINGERPICKING ROCK
00699716......$9.99

FINGERPICKING STANDARDS
00699613......$9.99

FINGERPICKING WEDDING
00699637......$9.99

FINGERPICKING WORSHIP
00700554......$7.99

FINGERPICKING NEIL YOUNG – GREATEST HITS
00700134......$12.99

FINGERPICKING YULETIDE
00699654......$9.99

FOR MORE INFORMATION, SEE YOUR LOCAL MUSIC DEALER,
OR WRITE TO:

HAL•LEONARD®
CORPORATION
7777 W. BLUEMOUND RD. P.O. BOX 13819 MILWAUKEE, WI 53213

Visit Hal Leonard online at **www.halleonard.com**

Prices, contents and availability subject to change without notice.

CELEBRATE CHRISTMAS
WITH YOUR GUITAR AND HAL LEONARD

THE BEST CHRISTMAS GUITAR FAKE BOOK EVER – 2ND EDITION

INCLUDES TAB

Over 150 Christmas classics for guitar. Songs include: Blue Christmas • The Chipmunk Song • Frosty the Snow Man • Happy Holiday • A Holly Jolly Christmas • I Saw Mommy Kissing Santa Claus • I Wonder As I Wander • Jingle-Bell Rock • Rudolph, the Red-Nosed Reindeer • Santa Bring My Baby Back (To Me) • Suzy Snowflake • Tennessee Christmas • and more.
00240053 Melody/Lyrics/Chords............................$19.95

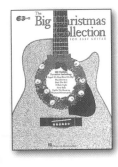

THE BIG CHRISTMAS COLLECTION FOR EASY GUITAR

Includes over 70 Christmas favorites, such as: Ave Maria • Blue Christmas • Deck the Hall • Feliz Navidad • Frosty the Snow Man • Happy Holiday • A Holly Jolly Christmas • Joy to the World • O Holy Night • Silver and Gold • Suzy Snowflake • and more. Does not include TAB.
00698978 Easy Guitar..$16.95

CHRISTMAS

 INCLUDES TAB

Guitar Play-Along Volume 22
Book/CD Pack

8 songs: The Christmas Song (Chestnuts Roasting on an Open Fire) • Frosty the Snow Man • Happy Xmas (War Is Over) • Here Comes Santa Claus (Right Down Santa Claus Lane) • Jingle-Bell Rock • Merry Christmas, Darling • Rudolph the Red-Nosed Reindeer • Silver Bells.
00699600 Guitar Tab..$15.95

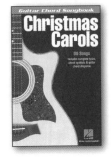

CHRISTMAS CAROLS

Guitar Chord Songbook

80 favorite carols for guitarists who just need the lyrics and chords: Angels We Have Heard on High • Away in a Manger • Deck the Hall • Good King Wenceslas • The Holly and the Ivy • Irish Carol • Jingle Bells • Joy to the World • O Holy Night • Rocking • Silent Night • Up on the Housetop • Welsh Carol • What Child Is This? • and more.
00699536 Lyrics/Chord Symbols/Guitar Chord Diagrams........$12.95

CHRISTMAS CAROLS

 INCLUDES TAB

Guitar Play-Along Volume 62
Book/CD Pack

8 songs: God Rest Ye Merry, Gentlemen • Hark! The Herald Angels Sing • It Came upon the Midnight Clear • O Come, All Ye Faithful (Adeste Fideles) • O Holy Night • Silent Night • We Three Kings of Orient Are • What Child Is This?
00699798 Guitar Tab..$12.95

CHRISTMAS CAROLS

INCLUDES TAB

Jazz Guitar Chord Melody Solos

Chord melody arrangements in notes & tab of 26 songs of the season. Includes: Auld Lang Syne • Deck the Hall • Good King Wenceslas • Here We Come A-Wassailing • Joy to the World • O Little Town of Bethlehem • Toyland • We Three Kings of Orient Are • and more.
00701697 Solo Guitar..$12.99

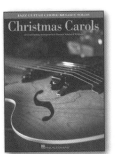

CHRISTMAS SONGS

Guitar Chord Songbook

80 Christmas favorites, including: Baby, It's Cold Outside • The Chipmunk Song • The Christmas Shoes • The Christmas Song • Grandma Got Run over by a Reindeer • Happy Holiday • I've Got My Love to Keep Me Warm • It Must Have Been the Mistletoe (Our First Christmas) • Miss You Most at Christmas Time • Silver Bells • We Need a Little Christmas • and more.
00699537 Lyrics/Chord Symbols/Guitar Chord Diagrams..........$12.95

CLASSICAL GUITAR CHRISTMAS COLLECTION

 INCLUDES TAB

Includes classical guitar arrangements in standard notation and tablature for more than two dozen beloved carols: Angels We Have Heard on High • Auld Lang Syne • Ave Maria • Away in a Manger • Canon in D • The First Noel • I Saw Three Ships • Joy to the World • O Christmas Tree • O Holy Night • Silent Night • What Child Is This? • and more.
00699493 Guitar Solo..$9.95

FINGERPICKING CHRISTMAS

INCLUDES TAB

Features 20 classic carols for the intermediate-level guitarist. Includes: Away in a Manger • Deck the Hall • The First Noel • It Came upon the Midnight Clear • Jingle Bells • O Come, All Ye Faithful • Silent Night • We Wish You a Merry Christmas • What Child Is This? • and more.
00699599 Solo Guitar..$8.95

FINGERPICKING CHRISTMAS CLASSICS

INCLUDES TAB

15 favorite holiday tunes, with each solo combining melody and harmony in one superb fingerpicking arrangement. Includes: Christmas Time Is Here • Feliz Navidad • I Saw Mommy Kissing Santa Claus • Mistletoe and Holly • My Favorite Things • Santa Baby • Somewhere in My Memory • and more.
00701695 Solo Guitar..$7.99

FINGERPICKING YULETIDE

INCLUDES TAB

Carefully written for intermediate-level guitarists, this collection includes an introduction to fingerstyle guitar and 16 holiday favorites: Do You Hear What I Hear • Happy Xmas (War Is Over) • A Holly Jolly Christmas • Jingle-Bell Rock • Rudolph the Red-Nosed Reindeer • and more.
00699654 Fingerstyle Guitar................................$9.99

THE ULTIMATE CHRISTMAS GUITAR SONGBOOK

100 songs in a variety of notation styles, from easy guitar and classical guitar arrangements to note-for-note guitar tab transcriptions. Includes: All Through the Night • Auld Lang Syne • Away in a Manger • Blue Christmas • The Chipmunk Song • The Gift • I've Got My Love to Keep Me Warm • Jingle Bells • One Bright Star • Santa Baby • Silver Bells • Wonderful Christmastime • and more.
00700185 Multi-Arrangements................................$19.95

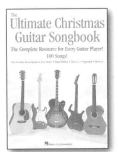

FOR MORE INFORMATION, SEE YOUR LOCAL MUSIC DEALER, OR WRITE TO:

HAL•LEONARD®
CORPORATION
7777 W. BLUEMOUND RD. P.O. BOX 13819 MILWAUKEE, WI 53213

www.halleonard.com

Prices, contents and availability subject to change without notice.

0711